THE
POWER
of
PROMOTIONAL
PRODUCTS

"How to Motivate Prospects, Reward Performance and Create Targeted Promotions with Residual Value..."

by DAVID BLAISE
& MARIA CARLTON

Edited by Tonia Cook Kimbrough

The Power of Promotional Products

ISBN: 0-9741003-1-5

Printed in the United States of America

David
"This book is dedicated to Andrew & Sarah, who teach me
the meaning of unconditional love, every day."

Maria
"For Nicholas and Alexander -
the best kids ever, I love you guys *Heaps!*"

Contents

Acknowledgements

This book would never have happened without the literary matchmaking skills of Christine Lovell at ASI whose vision bridged two continents. I would like to thank my coauthor Maria Carlton for her extreme patience and openness in allowing this project to evolve as it has.

I am grateful for the participation of Tonia Cook Kimbrough whose contributions far exceed the editing for which she is credited, Vytas Masalaitis who brought clarity to art and setup, and Brenda Webster "The Great Brendini" for working her magic on the cover.

Special thanks to Tom and Jean Fry for their unwavering confidence and encouragement, Rick Drake, my partner in business and Claire Blaise, my partner in life. What a long, strange trip it's been...

David Blaise

Thanks to everyone who helped to make this happen, and especially to the pre-press experts, printers, embroiderers and engravers who all contributed their expertise and ideas; and to the marketers, clients and suppliers who we have known along the way that have helped to ensure accuracy of the technical and nontechnical terms and explanations in this book.

I'd also like to thank Ross Beaton of Logo Line, Australia and Chris Lovell at ASI, because without their enthusiasm for this project and Ross referring me to Chris, who in turn introduced me to David, this would not have been possible to do. A special thanks to you David for all you've done.

This book has evolved with the help of many international phone calls, emails and is proof that two people who have never even sat around a table can create something like this so successfully.

Maria Carlton

Introduction

Some Marketers Just Don't Get It

It's incredible but true. Many people, including those who consider themselves to be truly sophisticated marketers, completely fail to understand or harness the power of promotional products.

Those who talk about handouts, giveaways, trinkets, tchotchkes, knickknacks, swag, or even "stuff" have completely missed the boat.

Many who *think* they understand the full capability of this marketing medium often overlook key applications and opportunities that could improve their results and increase their bottom lines dramatically!

Sure, all the usual thinking about branding, recognition, good will and motivation is fine. But let's forget about that for a moment. How about a more aggressive goal for your next promotional campaign?

Make All Your Marketing and Advertising More Accountable!

Believe it or not, promotional products hold the key to quantifying the performance of every marketing medium you use. In short, you can use them to keep all of your other advertising honest!

Let's face it, the days of major ego advertising and blowing money for the sheer thrill of seeing our company name advertised on TV, cable or the Internet are now largely behind us. Sure, a few companies still manage to squander budgets on massive, unproven advertising and branding campaigns, but today, most companies are forced to insist on *getting results*.

7

Promotional products allow advertisers to know, without a doubt, what's working in their advertising arsenal and what isn't.

Eliminate the Waste

Run a television, radio or newspaper ad and it will cost you the same, whether it generates one lead or one thousand. But when you use any of these media to motivate a new prospect or client to *take action now* in order to receive a promotional gift... response rates rise dramatically!

In fact, if they don't, it's a strong indication that your existing marketing may not be working as well as you think!

In this book, we'll explore The Power of Promotional Products. Learn how to get the best results for your time and money. Discover the four factors of a powerful promotion and get good, solid, action-oriented recommendations on how to harness that power for the lifetime benefit of your business.

Here's to your success!

Chapter One

What Are Promotional Products and Why Are They So Popular?

The Power of Promotional Products comes from their ability to get an effective, targeted marketing message in front of exactly the prospects and clients you need to reach, and *keep it there...* without the waste associated with other media.

While broadly considered to be any useful item featuring a company logo, name or advertising message, the very best promotional products don't just brand, they generate actual, measurable results.

The Four Factors of Successful Promotions

1. **Audience-appropriate product.** The most compelling marketing message in the world will be lost on the recipient if the promotional item itself is not appropriate to the targeted audience.
2. **Effective marketing message.** Too often, promotional products convey only company names or logos without any strong benefit statement, advantage or call to action. It generally costs no more to add these things to the imprint, but the effect it can have on the entire campaign is dramatic.
3. **Targeted, qualified recipients.** Very few companies can afford to market to everyone. So each promotion should be geared toward the individuals most likely to generate positive results for you.

4. **The right time.** It's been said that the difference between salad and garbage is timing. This is equally true of marketing. The perfect marketing message delivered either too soon or too late will not produce the desired result.

However, when you imprint an audience-appropriate product with an effective marketing message and deliver it to a qualified group of recipients at the right time, you dramatically increase your likelihood of success. The best promotional products advisors in the world are those who help their clients to master the four factors of successful promotions.

Which Products are Most Popular?

There are over 650,000 items offered by promotional products suppliers, providing a wealth of choices to fit your target audience and message. So, which items are most popular? According to the Promotional Products Association International (PPAI), the top product categories sold by promotional products advisors are:

Wearables	29.3%
Writing Instruments	10.6%
Desk/Office/Business Accessories	7.6%
Calendars	7.0%
Bags	5.9%
Glassware/Ceramics	5.5%
Recognition Awards/Watches & Clocks/Trophies/Emblematic Jewelry	4.0%
Magnets/Buttons/Badges/Ribbons/Stickers	3.5%
Automotive Accessories	3.5%
Sporting Goods/Leisure Products/Travel Acc.	3.3%
Computer Products	3.1%

Other	2.9%
Games/Toys/Playing Cards/Inflatables	2.6%
Housewares/Tools	2.6%
Textiles	2.4%
Electronic Devices/Phonecards	2.3%
Personal Pocket/Purse Products	2.2%
Food Gifts	1.7%

According to data compiled by both the Advertising Specialty Institute (ASI) and Promotional Products Association International (PPAI), this was roughly a $15.6 billion dollar industry in the United States in 2002, up from $9.4 billion in 1996—a 60% increase.

How to Reap the Rewards of "Residual Marketing"

Promotional products are a cost-effective way to reach and to motivate key decision-makers. First, they get in front of them. Second, and perhaps most importantly, they *remain in front of them.*

Direct mail illustrates the value. When you prospect, or contact a client by mail and include a free gift or promotional item, you increase the likelihood that the package will get opened and generate a response. A 1992 study by Silver Marketing Group for PPAI found that the response rate was 75% higher than that of those who received a sales letter only. But getting your message in front of the prospect is just the first step.

After the package is opened, the promotional product *continues to work,* creating *ongoing advertising* in addition to a positive feeling about your company. It is a tangible reminder that remains long after the letter has been filed. We call this benefit "residual marketing."

For example, when you leave a note pad or other usable item with your client, every time he or she uses it and sees your logo, it re-enforces your brand to him or her. Ideally it is also there at a point of decision-making, when the prospect is most in need of the service or product you offer.

Perhaps the most significant reason for the popularity of promotional products is the frequency of exposure and reasonable cost per impression.

An article in the Wall Street Journal said that a coffee mug with an imprinted marketing message may be seen by the designated recipient as often as five times a day. Could you afford to reach a prospect using television five times a day? What about radio? Or even newspaper?

If an imprinted note pad has 100 sheets, you can expect a bare-bones minimum of 100 impressions. If each note is then passed to just one other person, it doubles the exposure. But the advertising and the impressions don't stop there. They continue for as long as the items remain in use or in sight.

Multiple impressions generate brand awareness, which is one of the keys to increased market share. And increased market share is one of the keys to success in any business.

Chapter Two

Does Your Promotion Have a Purpose?

Some companies use promotional products as "handouts" or "giveaways." And while that may be adequate for some, this book is about The Power of Promotional Products, and quite frankly, giveaways are *not* where the power lies…

The myopic view that promotions and giveaways are the same thing, likely costs businesses untold millions of dollars each year. Because for many marketing savvy companies, it doesn't make sense to simply give away items. But it *does* make sense to create effective promotions. And effective promotions begin with a purpose.

Giveaways vs. Promotions

Let's say a car dealer contacts a typical promotional products distributor about ordering 1,000 key tags to give out to 1,000 people within a five mile radius of her dealership. Since this distributor may not have been trained on The Power of Promotional Products, he simply replies, "what color?" The dealer says, "red." The key tags are ordered, delivered, given out to 1,000 people within a five mile radius of the dealership, and not surprisingly, nothing happens!

Now let's say that same car dealer contacts a true promotional products *advisor* about ordering 1,000 key tags to give out to 1,000 people within a five mile radius of her dealership. This advisor understands The Power of Promotional Products. So instead of asking, "what color," he asks, "why do you want to do that?"

The car dealer explains that she's trying to get recognition among the people in her neighborhood. She wants them to come in and take a test drive. She also thinks it would be great if some of them would actually buy a car from her. These three things are the purpose of the promotion. 1. Get recognition, 2. Encourage test drives and 3. Sell some cars.

Based on that information, the promotional products advisor may recommend the following: "Let's send out the same 1,000 key tags to the same 1,000 people. But let's attach a key to the key tag and let them know that if they come into the dealership within a certain amount of time (say thirty days), they can try the key in a car that is parked inside the dealership. If the key opens the car, they win a prize." Could be a dashboard cell phone holder, a travel mug, or it could be a new car, depending on the car dealer's budget. "Anyone who comes in and takes a test drive will get their choice of a custom imprinted back seat organizer or a CD holder. Those that buy a car will also receive an exclusive pair of driving gloves as a thank you gift.

"Now you have a promotion instead of a giveaway. At the end of the promotion, you can say, 'we sent out 1,000 key tags and forty seven people came in to try their key in the car. Of those forty seven, twenty took a test drive and six bought a new car. The average purchase price was $24,000.00, so the promotion generated $144,000.00 in sales.' That sure beats a giveaway, doesn't it?"

The Promotion Makes All the Difference

Those who don't understand The Power of Promotional Products will often settle for a giveaway. But when it doesn't work, they'll likely blame the item they used, the distributor they purchased from, the state of the economy, market conditions or promotional products in general.

"Yes," they'll say, "we tried promotional products and they just don't work for us." Most will never realize that it didn't work because there was no reason for it to work. There was no purpose to the promotion. And in fact, there wasn't even a promotion. Just a giveaway. Big difference.

This is not to say "don't do giveaways." There is much to be said for giving a gift of obligation to someone that you wish to motivate. But go in with your eyes open. If your purpose is to simply create impressions, a giveaway can do that. However, if the purpose is to attract attention, motivate prospects to action and sell more of your products and services, you will likely require a targeted promotion rather than a simple giveaway.

What is Your Purpose?

When considering a promotion, begin with your purpose in mind. A great way to do this is to start by asking yourself the following key questions and telling your promotional advisor the answers:

1. **What is the purpose of the promotion?** What am I looking to accomplish? Do I want to get attention and create awareness? Or do I want to accomplish more? Am I interested in rewarding performance? Motivating someone to do something? If so, what specific action do I want them to take? What do I want them to *do*?

Promotional products are great at getting people to do things! They can be used to dramatically improve your existing lead generation efforts and get new prospects to contact you. They can be used to retain existing clients or reactivate those who haven't ordered in a while. Promotional products can be used as an incentive to encourage someone to do a good job. Or they can be used to reward a job well done. Any of these are valid purposes that begin to demonstrate The Power of Promotional Products.

2. Who, specifically, do I want to impact with my promotion? Effective promotions depend upon effective targeting, and unlike

other media, there is little to no waste with promotional products, since they can be delivered only to the specific individuals you choose.

How do you suppose the results of our key tag promotion would differ, if targeted to the following groups:
- 1,000 drivers with five to seven year old cars.
- 1,000 drivers with two to four year old cars.
- 1,000 non-drivers who radically oppose the use of combustion engines.

Same promotion. Dramatically different results.

3. What exactly do I want to communicate to my targeted group? Like *Mr. Ed*, the talking horse in the classic television series, you should never speak unless you have something to say. However, many businesses still "wing it," rather than taking the time to compose a strong, effective marketing message.

How would the results of our key tag promotion differ with the use of the following messages?
- "Joe's Motors: Free parts and labor with your new car purchase for twelve months."
- "Joe's Motors: Reliable service since 1979."
- "Joe's Motors: No personal checks. No credit cards. All sales final."

While these examples may seem extreme, they demonstrate the importance of the message. Some people imprint promotional products with just a logo. That's the equivalent of saying only "Joe's Motors." Not exactly inspiring, is it?

As you think your promotion through, consider including a strong, compelling benefit statement. If it's printed in the same color as your logo, it generally doesn't cost any more, but it can improve your results dramatically.

4. Where do I want to reach my targeted group? Another

tremendous advantage of promotional products over other media, is that in addition to choosing *who* to reach, you can also choose *where*. Where will my prospect be most receptive to my message? At work? At a trade show? In the car? Does my prospect work in an office? At a desk? In a cubicle? Or on a tractor in the middle of a field? With over half a million products, you can promote yourself virtually anywhere. Would I rather reach my prospect at home? If so, in which room? How about a custom imprinted TV remote for the den? Or a magnet for the kitchen? With imprinted soaps, sponges or washcloths, you could literally market to someone in the shower! Of course, a professionally trained promotional advisor can help you to determine which products will get your message in front of your prospect, wherever you choose to reach them.

5. **How will I get it into their hands?** Will we distribute our product at trade shows, in person or via direct mail? Will we deliver it ourselves, by our sales representatives or via courier? Whatever you choose, the delivery method is part of the overall experience, and should be considered carefully. Presenting the recipient with a gift-wrapped present in person creates a completely different experience than if the same gift arrives in a brown corrugated box via UPS.

6. **When do you want to start getting the results of your promotion?** Whether your purpose is to motivate your salespeople, enhance morale, improve safety in the work place or recognize your best clients, when do you want to start accomplishing that? Now or three months from now?

When you have a good, solid purpose for your promotion, you will notice that you are far more likely to want to get started right away. While it may seem okay to put off buying bright yellow t-shirts and reflective hats, it probably seems less okay to put off implementation of your warehouse safety program. (Ironically, that program may consist solely of bright yellow shirts and reflective hats!) But once again, the purpose drives the promotion.

Chapter Three

Managing Your Options

One of the first things you'll discover about this highly effective form of advertising is that your options are virtually unlimited! Not only are there hundreds of thousands of products, there are hundreds of ways of combining, printing, using and presenting each one.

This book is designed to help you to get the most from this targeted media so that you no longer view promotional products as mere "handouts" or "giveaways," but rather as cost-effective methods for tracking results and getting your marketing message in front of exactly the people who need to see it… on a repetitive basis.

This chapter looks at some of the options available to you as an advertiser; how they work together; how you can use promotional products as an important part of your marketing mix, and why they work so well for those who take the time to understand their function.

Promotional Products in Relation to Other Marketing Options

The objective of advertising and promotion is to get results, create awareness… and to leave traces. Magazines, newspapers, radio, TV, billboards, yellow pages, promotional products and direct mail are some of the most commonly recognized methods to advertise your name, message or special offer. Other methods include signs, banners, flyers, circulars, advertising on buses, shelters, automobiles, messages flown behind airplanes and traditional word of mouth.

The marketing objective of every company is to successfully

brand itself, in order to sell more of its products or services.

Marketing = Branding

Selecting the Best Marketing Methods to Use

Prior to choosing the most suitable media, advertisers must consider their primary and secondary target markets (who they want to target), reach (the number of people they are reaching), frequency (the frequency with which they reach those people), and of course, cost.

Other considerations include the length of the campaign. Long campaigns may be designed to ensure that people know who, what and where you are, while a short intensive campaign may be used to sell products within a given time frame.

First – decide on your preferred media options.

Research suggests that in order to deliver your advertising message effectively, recipients need to hear or see the advertisement a minimum of three times (and perhaps as may as eight or nine times) before they will be ready to respond to it.

Most media attempt to offer you access to their audience. For varying levels of cost, they will put together a marketing plan to deliver a certain number of eyes and ears to see and hear what you have to offer. Some will recommend running your advertisement for days, others weeks and still others months or years.

The following "mainstream media" are established and proven. Each has its own particular strengths and weaknesses.

Newspapers

For example, a newspaper advertisement with potential to reach

150,000 readers (of whom, only 1,500 may actually be prospects for your products and services), may require 2 to 5 ads, at a cost of $500 to $1500 per ad.

We know that the targeted reader will most likely need to be exposed to your message more than once before he or she will be ready to respond to it. But newspapers tend to be read either in the morning or evening, and not necessarily at a time that will result in an immediate response.

In addition, today's newspaper is tomorrow's birdcage liner, so the window of opportunity for response can be relatively short.

Radio

Radio is more likely to be heard regularly through the day, perhaps at times that are more conducive to getting people to respond to your message. Radio is instant. If something is happening (whether locally or internationally) you are very likely to hear about it on the radio. If you hear a rumor, you may listen to the news at the top of the hour to check out the story. In this way, radio is a recognized source of news and information.

However, in order for radio to be effective, you need to be sure that your message is simple, has impact, and is heard often enough to reach your targeted market. By often enough, I mean at least 3 times a day. To ensure that happens, you may need to schedule at least 5 to 8 advertisements per day (depending on timing), to allow for the times that listeners are busy or away from their radio.

Essentially, this means that a successful radio campaign may need as many as 10 commercials per day, over several days or weeks to be truly effective, at a cost of hundreds or even thousands of dollars per day, depending upon the size of your market. And while a radio station may offer you access to 100,000 listeners, you may find that only a few dozen are good prospects for what you have to offer. This is particularly true of business-to-business marketers who offer a highly specialized product.

For example, how many people listening to the radio in any given day have the need for a high capacity copier? Perhaps some, but will it be enough to justify the cost of reaching tens of thousands of non-prospects as well?

Both radio and newspaper are essentially short-term advertising options that must have an immediate effect, and be run continuously in order to generate consistent results.

Television

Television advertising can be very effective, but it costs quite a bit to create and schedule an effective television ad. If it is part of your marketing plan, and you are able to maintain the high cost of production and repeated airing, then it may be worthwhile for you. However, even in this case, supporting television with at least one other form of advertising is recommended.

Television viewers often "tune out" either physically or mentally during commercials. They do this by channel surfing, talking, leaving the room or even editing out ads when recording a favorite program. For this reason, broadcasters are increasingly beginning to offer "product placements," a subtle type of advertising, which includes a company's logo or product as part of the action within the program itself.

Big companies like Pepsi and McDonalds are now able to do this as a way to increase brand awareness – but this is far too expensive to be a practical option for local car dealers, banks or furniture retailers.

Note: Sponsorship of radio and television programs on a long term basis can be a great brand building option for the marketers who can afford it, but the cost can be high and responsiveness is nearly impossible to track without specific procedures in place.

Billboards

A billboard will typically appear for several weeks, and your message will be exposed to a certain number of motorists driving by. While billboards may help with branding, they are generally not very successful at getting an instant response to your message (unless the message happens to contain the words, "Exit Here!")

Yellow Pages

Yellow Pages may be a valuable tool if your buyer has already decided that he or she is in the market for your product or service. In this type of advertising, it is important to tell the buyer who you are, and why they should call you before they call any of the sixteen or so other similar companies that may be advertising on the same page.

With the increased use of web marketing, and the ability to directly link your online yellow pages advertisement to your own website, there are now many options to consider with this medium. However, in a printed book, you are only able to update your advertisement once a year. As a result, special promotions are out, as are any other time sensitive events.

Some marketers use radio or television to direct people to "see our ad in the local yellow pages." Unless yours is the only company of its kind advertising in the yellow pages, we think this is a very bad idea. Why would you direct potential prospects to a medium that surrounds your information with details and contact information for every one of your potential competitors?

Magazines

These are generally read when first purchased, although some may linger for a while (most notably in doctors offices!). Regardless of whether they are weekly, monthly, or quarterly, a typical magazine normally lasts only as long as it takes to be replaced by the next issue.

Magazines are often more targeted than other media, offering advertising that appeals directly to the market that buys or subscribes to it. For time sensitive promotions, you can target generally, although you never know when (or if) the magazine will actually be read. In addition, magazine advertising is often sold based on the number of copies printed, rather than sell-through figures. It is a seldom-known fact that some of the magazines appearing in bookstores and other retail outlets never sell out before the next issue arrives. In those cases, the front covers are torn off and returned to the publisher for credit, while the rest of the issue, including all those great ads, are thrown away by the store owner.

Direct Mail

As an advertiser, you want the best possible response, from the maximum number of clients to achieve the most cost effective outcome for your money. In the past, direct mail was considered a hit and miss option. Traditional direct mail provided a 1 to 3% response rate if you were lucky, and therefore could be very expensive and wasteful. However, smarter technology has lead to more effective forms of direct marketing, which can be improved even more dramatically with the use of promotional products.

Personalized direct mail, sent out to previous, existing and potential clients reaches people who already know who you are. As a result, they are much more likely to be receptive to your marketing. This can include everyone who has had some contact with your company during the past 6 months (such as suppliers, contractors, unsuccessful quote recipients, etc.) And while your direct mail might cost an average of $1.50 for each letter (including a small gift such as a refrigerator magnet), you will have a much better chance of striking the right note with existing contacts.

Even when sending direct mail to a targeted market that is not made up of existing contacts, if you include a promotional item that may be kept longer than the letter itself, it will likely increase your branding exposure, advertising impressions and your likelihood of success.

If the recipient doesn't respond to your letter or offer immediately, they will still likely keep the gift (with your name and marketing message on it), which keeps you in front of them and positions you to make the sale whenever they are ready to purchase the product you sell.

> **Many studies have demonstrated that sending a personal letter directly to your target market with a promotional product will increase the effectiveness of your direct mail campaign. Add a personal letter and targeted promotional product to your next mailing and test the results. You will very likely see an increase in readership and response over just a brochure or mailing piece alone.**

The Media Mix

Some of the media above work very well when used in conjunction with each other. For example, many mainstream advertisers rely on a combination of television, radio, newspaper, direct mail and promotional products. Those with more limited budgets may choose to limit their advertising to newspaper and local radio. However, nearly every campaign can benefit from the addition of targeted promotional products.

Billboards can work well to reinforce national products. Magazines can work well to reinforce national campaigns.

All of these options are useful for either short term campaigns or long term branding, assuming the advertiser has the budget to keep them going.

Please note: Every promotional campaign should have a clear set of objectives. You should know what you expect to get from sponsoring a sports team or major golf event, just as you should have specific expectations from placing a two-page color advertisement in your local newspaper. Sending 5,000 direct mail letters is something you would only do if you expected a good response and a reasonable return on your investment. Use promotional products as incentives to help increase response, then track the results to ensure that all your advertising is held to that same level of accountability.

Buying Trends

The average large ticket purchase takes approximately six weeks to close. (The higher the price the longer the process)

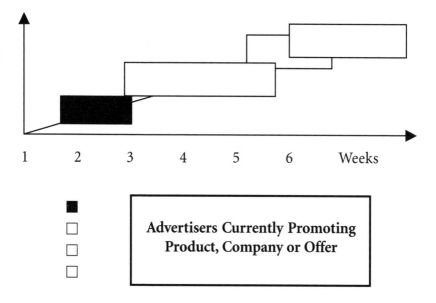

Advertisers Currently Promoting Product, Company or Offer

The client is most likely to buy from the advertisers marked by the white boxes. The company indicated by the black box runs the risk of missing out by no longer being "top of mind" when the client is ready to make the purchase.

The Process Over 6 Weeks

1. The clients first think about making a change.
2. They begin to notice advertising for the product.
3. They start to ask around, to find out what is available, where it is available… and the costs.
4. They begin looking in earnest.
5. They become emotionally involved with the desired purchase.
6. They purchase.

When you advertise a product, you are reaching individuals who may be in each of these stages. However, only those in stages 3 though 6 may be ready to buy! The others will be lost to you, unless you back up your short-term advertising with an ongoing campaign of branding or residual advertising.

One measure of advertising success is growth in the number of inquiries

Most advertisers:

Stop-start advertising and awareness.

Smart Advertisers:

Consistent, for increased awareness.

Contrary to the advice you may get from some advertising sales representatives, success is *not* "all about repetition." It is about repeating the things that work and eliminating the things that don't.

Test various media and use promotional products in your advertising as an incentive to get people to respond to your ad (for example, "stop by today and get a free sleeve of golf balls.") If enough people come in and ask for a free sleeve of golf balls, you can tell the media is able to pull for you. If no one comes in, test other media. Keep the ones that work and drop the ones that don't.

But please note, you must be sure that the promotional item you offer makes sense for your promotion. A free sleeve of golf balls is only attractive to golfers. Also, you don't want to use promotional products to attract "freebie-seekers." That is, people who have no interest in your product, but just want the free gift you're offering.

A skilled promotional products advisor can help you to put together a promotion that is both practical and functional.

A second, equally important measure of success is converting inquiries into sales

Getting qualified leads and inquiries is important, but it is just as important to be able to convert those leads into sales. Be sure to examine both your lead figures and your sales conversion rates before adapting your strategy. Some people think that their advertising is not working, when, in actuality, they are getting plenty of qualified leads, but their sales team is not able to convert those leads into sales. In those cases, you may consider using premiums to improve conversion, or perhaps additional sales training should be addressed.

Many companies work on building loyalty with their clients to remain "top of mind." For example, some automobile dealers offer great service, free inspections and add on benefits such as a free CD holder, driving gloves or sunglass holders. The car dealer's name and marketing message may be imprinted on the free gift as a subtle, but effective way of reinforcing brand and client loyalty. Many clients go back year after year for such service and bonuses, and skip price shopping entirely because the dealership succeeded in making them feel special and appreciated.

> **It really is easier and less expensive to retain the clients you already have, than to have to go out and find new clients to replace them.**

When used as recommended in this book, The Power of Promotional Products will get you the results you need and leave long-term traces of *your brand* with your prospects and clients. They are a constant reminder of you, your company, your service and ideally, their excellent experience with you.

Chapter Four

Some Types of Promotional Products and Gifts

With hundreds of thousands of promotional products available, it is impossible to list them all here. But the following is an overview of some popular choices and how they are best used.

Calendars, Diaries, Desk Pads and Wall Planners

Calendars have been a perennial favorite because of their interactive nature, usefulness, and the likelihood that they'll be seen by recipients on a daily basis. Few products match the frequency of exposure calendars provide, given that most people check their schedules several times a day, 365 days a year.

When choosing calendars as a promotional gift, consider what format is best for your recipients and the chances that your calendar will be kept and displayed if they happen to receive several that year.

Here is where it pays to keep your audience's tastes and behaviors in mind. First, what type of calendar would your audience find most useful? Calendars come in all shapes and sizes, from spiral wall calendars to tiny pocket planners. A desk diary may be more appropriate for an executive gift, whereas a wallet-sized calendar-card can make more sense for a mass, customer mailing.

If you want to be right under your clients' noses all year, then a desk pad might be a smart alternative. These are often a little more expensive than a standard calendar, but worth the extra dollars if you consider the value of having so much space to promote your products and the practical value to your clients.

A wall planner is still a very handy item to pin up on most office walls, despite the growing popularity of personal digital assistants (PDAs). Even the most advanced technology buffs with their electronic diaries tend to refer regularly to their large wall planner (the kind you can write all over is best) for getting a clear picture of things.

Small pocket diaries are a nice idea but rapidly being taken over as useful items by the increased popularity of PDAs. And diary giants like Franklin-Covey®, Dayrunner® and Daytimers® spend a lot of money heavily promoting their own products, which might render your lovely gift a distant second, and relegate it to your prospect's bottom drawer.

On the positive side, an advantage to diaries is that you can often customize the cover, the first few pages, or possibly every page in the book. If you use relevant information about your company or tips to improve your recipients' performance, then the diary becomes a valuable, useful asset beyond appointment keeping. For example, an agricultural company might include rainfall information, space for recording harvest information, and market prices, with a number of handy tips for getting better value out of products that their company supplies.

If you're not 100% sure that the diary, calendar, wall, or desk planner is going to be universally appreciated by your recipients, then either select an entirely different gift or create a smaller selection or combination of these that specifically target a varied audience's tastes and expectations. For example, a digitally printed set of wall planners, desk planners, and desk calendars might be designed especially for your company, then digitally printed in smaller quantities, and given as sets or individually (depending on each recipient).

Artwork is key factor in choosing a calendar as well. It's no good selecting a lovely landscape just because that is what you like, if the majority of your intended recipients are young males who may prefer something a bit sportier.

Many calendar suppliers will work with your promotional

products advisor to design a calendar especially for your company using images of your own products or something specific to your industry or target audience. Here again, the increasing popularity of digital printing means that you no longer have to produce thousands (or even hundreds) in order for this to be a cost-effective option.

Calendars also tend to be somewhat cyclical – some years it seems that everyone gives them away, while other years you're lucky to get one or two. What is predictable, however, is that calendars will be missed if you've traditionally given them to your clients and then decide to stop. Give your calendars out annually and early (at least two months before the new year begins) so that your target audience will look forward to and begin using them before they receive any other promotional calendars.

Writing Instruments

A look at your own desktop will probably reveal multiple pens and pencils, many logoed. There's a reason the promotional popularity of this medium has endured over the years, second only to imprinted apparel. Writing instruments are daily tools that recipients not only see, they *hold*—therefore increasing the time spent with the product, your logo and advertising message. Frequency of use is high and therefore cost-per-impression is low.

Your choices in writing instruments—including pens, pencils, highlighters and markers—range from the novel and inexpensive to the elegant and expensive. Some are designed for amusement, including flip-tops and bubbles, and others are equipped for multifunction offering a stylus, flashlight, etc. Here is where a trained promotional advisor can help you sort through the options to match your target audience to the item that will be most appropriate.

There are lots of beautiful pens in various styles that are based on trendy fashions rather than long-term quality. These are better at making an immediate statement than building lifetime loyalty.

While many people will admire and appreciate a funky bright pen that also writes well, not many will lose sleep over the subsequent loss of a plastic pen – regardless of how "fabulous" it is. However, there is a certain amount of memorable mileage gained from the original impression, and the pen will likely end up in another person's hands if lost by the original recipient.

Low cost (anything from $0.50 - $5.00) in a pen is best considered a promotional item – not a gift. In this case your objective is to give out lots of them, and hope they travel far and wide, with your company name/logo/message clearly there for all to see. One manufacturer's study showed that the average pen may have as many as eight owners, due to pass-along value or the fact that many people tend to inadvertently walk away with other people's pens.

Be careful to avoid giving away pens of questionable quality that look good but do not write well, or the type that only lasts a short time before running out of ink. This only serves to cheapen your company image.

On the other hand, if you want your clients to really appreciate a nice pen as a gift, then it pays to ensure that it both looks and writes like an expensive pen. If it's refillable, will your recipients be able to easily obtain refill cartridges? The best choice in a quality pen as a corporate gift is to go with a recognized brand, or a writing instruments that offers a lifetime guarantee—especially if you want your client to keep (and appreciate) it for a very long time.

The imprint itself will also affect the value of the pen in the recipients' minds. How you customize a pen depends somewhat on the style. A low-cost plastic option will look better if colorfully pad printed whereas the more expensive metal pen might be most suited to engraving or even printing tone on tone for a classy, embossed look. Personalization also serves to ensure the long-term value of a pen, as very few people will dispose of a pen (or anything else) that has their own name on it!

Key Rings

Think of the number of times a day that you use your keys. Now you can appreciate the amount of logo exposure that a good key tag can offer.

Some basic thinking needs to go into buying key tags. If you want your recipient to appreciate it for the long term, you'll need to spend a little more money and go for a good brass or leather option that will stand the test of time. If you are looking to appeal to a wider audience, you may select a less expensive alternative in plastic or acrylic. Either way, key tags offer a multitude of choices in function, style and price.

If your company is not in the vehicle, housing or security industry, would you still give away a key tag? While it's true that key tags make great gifts for companies for which they're clearly relevant, a clever promotional advisor knows this medium isn't limited to just those industries.

A variety of features and customization options open the door to many markets and audiences. A target base of accountants may appreciate a fob with a mini calculator attached. A local bank could emboss a leather key tag/coin purse with its name and phone number for incoming students at a nearby university; it might even throw in a few quarters for laundry. Or a consumer-products company may want materials die-cast or die-cut to create a key-tag replica for a new product launch.

Here is where it pays to review the four factors of promotional success: audience-appropriateness, marketing message, qualified recipients and timing—there are enough choices in key tags available to fit most any combination of those elements.

Mugs and Glassware

There are over 10,000 mugs and more than 7,000 glasses

available from promotional products suppliers, according to a recent search in the industry sourcing tool ESP. Quantity of choice alone makes this one of the most prolific product categories. There are metal commuter mugs, ceramic mugs, latte cups, ice-tea glasses, baby cups, liqueur glasses... the list goes on and on. Choosing the right mug or glassware for your promotion requires careful analysis of who will be drinking from it and where they'll be drinking. *What* they're drinking and *how much* might also play a role!

There are a few basic rules of thumb when giving away drinking vessels, one is that you can give away one mug, but glasses are best offered in sets (though it's not unheard of for a single glass to be given as a favor from a party or event). If your budget won't stretch to two glasses—nicely packaged and presented as an optional extra—consider giving a coffee or tea mug instead.

Also consider whether you want your recipients to take the glass or mug home. If you do, then customizing may need to be discreet. We tend to remember where we received a gift that is special, useful and attractive. As a result, we don't always need to see a company's signature or logo every time we bring it out of the cabinet.

On the other hand, a fun, funky printed mug is more likely to become favored at the office than at home, providing exposure to the user as well as his or her colleagues. Location of use is important in terms of propriety, as well. We'll use an imprinted coffee mug in the staff room, and sometimes at home, but very rarely will we do the same with a wine or beer glass, which may send the wrong message in an office environment.

Finally, quality is a must when giving ceramics and glassware; a broken mug handle, for example, can raise liability issues. Here is where a knowledgeable advisor can provide invaluable guidance. They know industry guidelines for safety and inspection, and can discern first quality from seconds.

Bags

Many people say – "I've got lots of bags, I don't really need anymore." However, these are often the same people who call and ask to borrow one when they go away for the weekend or camping. A useful promotional bag is "just the right size for…" something specific. Beach bags, tote bags and lap top bags spring to mind.

Fortunately, bags are available in every shape, color, style, and range in durability and reliability. Options range from basic totes in canvas, to leather briefcases that house computers, to youth-oriented backpacks in stylish PVC. Depending on the material, you can print, transfer, emboss or embroider on them. Not only are they highly visible, they travel! Yes, one thing you can count on is that a good bag will be seen in many places—from airports and gyms to bobbing on children's backs as they bike to school.

Insulated bags and wine carriers are popular options for people who like to give a bottle of wine at an event or end of year, but don't want the memory to fade with the last drop. Trade shows are another common arena for logoed bags; imprinted with a company name and booth number they become a walking billboard to draw prospect traffic to an exhibit.

Umbrellas and Other Mobile Billboards

Next time you're at a trade show, or watching any local sporting event, take a look around at how many imprinted umbrellas you see, or people wearing boldly printed jackets, caps and T-shirts.

You'll also likely see these same people standing beside a bag or carrying a back pack. And you would think that water bottles with company names on them must make the drinks taste better at half time, as they grossly outnumber the unprinted variety.

Play a game of golf, and you'll notice that the golf bags, balls, clothing, and all other accessories are emblazoned with printed messages and logos. This is due in part to the efforts of large sporting goods companies such as Nike and Reebok recognizing early on that getting their names "out there" where people are mobile, talking to each other, and doing healthy activities are great brand-associated events that offer huge marketing potential.

We're told that the average consumer is exposed to thousands (or even tens of thousands) of advertising messages every day. So it makes sense that when our clients are going to spend several hours on the golf course, exposing them to some very specific branding during that time is a great, subtle way of increasing awareness over all the other messages that they have encountered that day.

The trick is to make sure that the item on which your brand appears, is something that others will admire and hopefully want for themselves. We all like to be the owner of something that someone else wants – so making sure your own printed product is the object of a certain amount of envy will help to ensure that others realize that in order to get one – they must become your customer!

Corporate Apparel

Corporate apparel, like an imprinted T-shirt with matching cap, is a mobile advertisement for your company. Imprinted apparel makes up nearly one-third of promotional product sales, attesting to its popularity among advertisers and corporate gift-givers. Its versatility is one reason for this market share. Today there are styles, sizes and colors for most any taste, occasion or audience.

Many companies that have embraced casual dress codes have looked to corporate-approved, imprinted apparel to keep their staff acceptably and comfortably dressed. Industry apparel suppliers now offer coordinated lines of men's wear and women's wear. There are oxfords, golf shirts, sweater sets, vests, ties, chinos, skirts... even socks and shoes that can complete an office-inspired look.

Employees can present a unified appearance for retail or

hospitality environments. Salespeople can stand out as a clearly marked resource for information at trade shows. Blue-collar workers can be dressed for safety and high visibility at a work site.

But the trick to successfully dressing your employees, consumers or clients is research and planning. A consumer products company with a teen-appealing brand can very likely convince their customers to not only wear, but even purchase, brand-logoed apparel — therefore becoming willing, walking advertisements—but only if the garments are fashionable and speak to the intended wearer on an emotional level. Again, think of sporting goods companies like Nike or beverage brands like Pepsi and Coca-Cola. Teens wear apparel labeled with these brands because they identify with characteristics of the brand—something young, cool or all-American. The garment, therefore, must demonstrate those brand characteristics as well.

Trained and experienced promotional products advisors can help you to choose audience-appropriate apparel, and then build a collection that meets your needs for a range of sizes and occasions. They can also help sort through the myriad ways to imprint garments from screen-printing and embroidery to special effects techniques.

Office Accessories

If you are going to send a promotion or gift to someone who is an office dweller then you need to consider whether or not it will be received as a useful and valued item. Perhaps no other product category requires as much consideration regarding functionality, since desktop "real estate" is very valuable and extremely limited.

Look for products with a purpose that are appropriate to the office for which they're intended. For example, desk accessories for a mechanic might be quite different than those of a high-power executive. The former needs durable items that are easily cleaned (no fine Italian leather desk blotters here) and the latter would likely scoff at a hard plastic clipboard. Yet each office accessory has its place with the right audience.

There are so many things that come under the heading of office accessories that it helps to group them as desktop, mouse pads/computer-related and decorative/wall items.

Desktop Products

Desktop products include note pads/note holders, pens (which we have already covered), paperclip holders, paperweights, calculators, address books, etc. – all of which are available as inexpensive novelties or as serious and practical products.

Many suppliers offer coordinated lines of desktop items, allowing you to plan a "series" promotion. You can create an incentive program around a set of stylish desktop products, gifting one each time a client makes a purchase or an employee reaches a goal. Once the recipient has collected the complete set, he or she is far more likely to favor your desktop gifts over others, because they present a tidy, coordinated look.

If you're going to give your clients a desk product – think hard about whether or not it looks good and will make a statement. Is it something that they will actually appreciate and use? Don't make determinations like this solely on budget. If something stays in front of your client for a long time, you will get much better residual marketing value than from a less expensive item that disappears quickly.

Mouse Pads/Computer-Related Items

Mouse pads tend to be much the same. If you see a mouse pad on a desk that looks worn or is too thick, you can guarantee the next one that arrives as part of someone else's promotion is going to replace it – fast! Mouse pads are not the sort of product we always buy for ourselves, so often we're willing to wait for the next promotional pad to turn up. We only keep those we really like, or those that seem to be very expensive and therefore appeal to our appreciation of luxury.

The great thing about mouse pads is that there is so much room to print on them. You can get your whole message, the name and address of your company, logo and picture of your product and still have room to put the mouse in the middle. This is why they hold so much appeal as effective promotional products. However, don't make the mistake of assuming that your average CEO is going to appreciate the same brightly printed mouse pad on his or her solid mahogany desk that a young receptionist might love.

There are many different variations of quality and materials used for mouse pads – an embossed leather one will cost a lot more than rubber-backed plastic, but for your upper management clients, the leather may enjoy a much longer life than the plastic. By the same token, sending the purchasing officer a new mouse pad every six months with your specials listed above your phone number can get your message across and ensure that he or she will enjoy the use of *your* new mouse pad. (At least as long as it takes to give you some orders.) Or you can send mouse pads imprinted with a calendar on an annual basis, upping their potential utility value and life-span.

Personalization also ensures that your mouse pad is front and center. Digitally imprinted mouse pads can be run in small quantities with your clients' own names on them, just for added impact during a promotion... imagine how much recipients will appreciate the extra thought you put into the gift.

Other computer-related items include screen savers, disk holders, note holders that stick on your computer, screen dusters, keyboard brushes, laptop bags, wrist rests, stress balls and novelty squeeze toys to use while browsing the Net. Some promotional product companies specialize in just computer accessories. Again, it's best to consider who your recipient is, and how likely they are to use what you might send them. For example, is your target audience likely to have a computer at their desks?

> **Employing a savvy promotional products advisor to counsel you on your choices, how the available products will suit your audience, and the best method of delivery is generally your *best* option. Can you search for products on your own? Of course, but trained, experienced promotional advisors more than pay for themselves by saving you an enormous amount of time, energy and effort.**

Decorative/Wall Items

The final category of office accessories is decorative items for the desk and wall. Clocks, executive toys, stress-relief items, photo frames, etc., are examples.

If you consider giving a clock to anyone, beware that in many cultures, including Asian, European, Celtic, and followers of the increasingly popular practice of Feng Shui, the gift of a time piece may make a negative impression. It can mean that you wish to hasten the meeting, or that you are giving away the value of your time with that person. Or in the case of giving to someone older than you are – it may just be considered generally insulting.

Some cultures teach that a way to counteract the "bad luck" associated with giving away time is to accept a coin in return, as a token gesture indicating that you accept that they are "buying" that gift from you (of course that may very well defeat the promotional approach you were looking for to begin with!)

In the United States, however, many businesspeople live by the clock, so a timepiece may be very appropriate. If you decide to give a clock, one that sits on a desk is a popular option. A useful idea is to offer one with a photo frame or card holder attached, so that it is even more practical. A wall clock is also a good idea, as it is unobtrusive but useful, and tends to be viewed often in an average day by everyone in the room, not just the recipient.

> **It is best not to give a clock, or watch**
> **unless you are *sure* that it will be well received.**

A more generally appreciated gift might be a business-card holder, photo holder, calculator or pen. Whatever you give, if it's something that is going to sit on someone's desk, your best option is to give a gift that is of very good quality. People are quick to complain about calculators that don't work or metal frames that quickly tarnish.

And always remember to always provide fresh batteries in any products that require them.

Tools and Household Effects

As with office accessories, this category of products is vast. Let's consider a few popular items. Swiss army knives and Leatherman tools are often considered some of the most welcomed gifts for men, as are flashlights and mini tool kits. However, women also love getting these things as gifts, and some women say they would be totally lost without the Victorinox® on their key rings.

Such tools are easy gifts to give and always appreciated as practical things that most people will keep and use for a very long time.

In some cultures, it is also considered bad luck (or in bad taste) to give a knife as a gift. As a result, we recommend against such promotional products in Asian countries. In Scotland, a gift of a knife is said to be an indication that you wish to cut the ties of friendship, unless a coin is offered with it.

Small tool sets for the car, kitchen or office, waiting for that moment when you need a small-job screwdriver, are a handy idea to many. But unless you expect that the set will be used quite regularly, serving as a good branding carrier, there may be better options to consider.

A manicure set, for example, will most likely be kept in a bathroom and used by various family members several times a month – and most sets like this will bear a logo, name or message very well. Likewise, a first-aid kit may be a good idea.

While there are some good recommendations and many types of promotional products outlined here – the primary message of this chapter is that there are so many thousands of ideas and variations of products, working with a trained promotional products advisor will help to ensure that you consider the appropriate range of options.

He or she can also help you to better apply the four factors of successful promotions when making your selection. Even the best of products fall short of spectacular results if they aren't audience appropriate, fail to carry the most effective marketing message or are distributed at the wrong time to someone other than a smartly targeted decision-maker.

Chapter Five

How to Balance Budget, Quality and Quantity

There is much more to buying promotional products than just liking how your logo looks on something. There are decisions to be made about the quality of the products, how many you need, how they'll be distributed and, of course, how much you are prepared to spend on them. Each of these issues relates directly back to the four factors of successful promotions:

Audience Appropriate

Would you send a low-quality pen to a high-power executive? Audience-appropriateness will certainly affect the quality of your product selection, and therefore your budget.

Effective Marketing Message

Does the combination of item and imprint effectively convey your marketing message? An incomplete or ineffective marketing message can do more harm than good. Does the selected item lend itself to advancing your company position and marketing message? What is the ideal imprinting technique for the product and what will that cost?

Targeted Recipients

Who is your targeted, qualified group of recipients? Are they the decision makers? How many recipients make up that group?

This will determine how much you can afford to spend per product.

Right Timing

How will you reach your target audience and when? Remember that the success of your promotion is dependent upon presentation and timing. Consider for a moment that sending a bulky gift, however fancy, via third class mail makes a much different impression than delivering it via overnight courier, or delivering it yourself. In addition, delays in bulk mail could negatively impact your campaign by reaching your target audience *after* the point of a critical purchasing decision or event. Therefore, the product you choose—its budget, quality, size, etc.—has as much to do with presentation, distribution method and timing, as with the audience itself.

Examining Some Scenarios

Clearly, there are many decisions to be made regarding budget, quality and quantity. This chapter looks at a few ways to make this process easier. Subsequent chapters address the demographics and psychographics of your audience, how to relate your brand values to your product choice, and other important criteria. First, however, let's consider a few scenarios with a $2,000 product budget:

• One dollar per item on 2,000 units, which might stay in the hands of some of your prospects or clients for a few days

• Fifty cents per item on 4,000 units, which might reach 4,000 potential new clients

• Ten dollars per item on a quality gift for your Top 200 clients, thanking them for their continued patronage

• Or twenty dollars for your Top 40 clients (and $7.50 for the remaining 160)

The return on your investment is measured against the value of the promotional products and will help you decide how best to apportion your budget.

Is your gift a way of building on existing client relationships to increase sales? Or is it a mass-market attention-grabber designed to capture leads?

Let's take a moment now to address a popular misconception: The one dollar gift to 2,000 prospects isn't necessarily a poor quality product that won't deliver leads. Neither can you assume that the $20 gift chosen for your top forty clients is going to outlast the pyramids or motivate your clients to buy more products and services from you. Sometimes a product is less expensive not because of poor quality or lack of effectiveness, but because of economies of scale that a supplier has achieved. On the flipside, higher expense may be a factor of markup due to operating costs and marketing, rather than an indication of the product's materials or workmanship.

A trained promotional products advisor knows how to discern the value and quality of products, regardless of their price points. He or she can help guide you to make decisions based on how a product is constructed and whether or not the materials themselves are of high quality. Many advisors have actually visited supplier plants and know first-hand of their quality-inspection processes, reliability, guarantee structures, etc. They may also know the probable frequency of exposure that each product type yields, and can help you compare cost per impression for your product options.

How a product is imprinted may also affect your budget. For instance, if you have the choice of a five dollar pen or an eight dollar calculator, both may be good options, but the five dollar pen might suit the budget and the overall project better than the more expensive calculator. If you prefer the calculator, however, printing it in one color instead of four colors may reduce the cost of the item by as much as two dollars each, and therefore bring the costs into line with your budget. Also, the calculator may have a larger imprint area, allowing you to include a tagline in addition to your company logo.

Table A - Thinking About Products

Here are a few questions to consider when deciding which types of promotional products to use for your marketing:

	Yes	No	Maybe
Do I want many low cost items?			
Do I want fewer, high quality, higher priced options?			
Do I need a large imprint area to accommodate more than just a logo?			
Does the product need to last for more than a few days?			
Will it be distributed by hand?			
Will it be sent via overnight courier?			
Will it be mailed?			
Is my company and project suited to fun or unusual novelty items?			
Is the item likely to get in front of and remain in front of the decision maker?			
Should I be conservative in my approach?			
Do I want the recipient to keep the product for himself or herself?			
Do I want the recipient to pass the item on to someone else after the message has been read?			
Does it matter if the item breaks or looks worn after the campaign is finished?			
Should the item itself be useful and practical?			
Does the item need to prompt an action from the recipient?			
Does the item have sufficient perceived value to prompt such an action?			
Will the item be used to test the effectiveness of other media (i.e. print, radio or TV) and be used as part of a larger, integrated campaign?			

Your answers will help to give you and your promotional products advisor a clearer idea of how to allocate your budget.

Table B - Working from a Budget

Sometimes the easiest way to approach a project is to work backwards from the budget

Example:

A. What is your maximum budget?	$2000	
B. How many items do you need?	100	
C. Are all recipients 100% the same? (If yes, available dollars per item = A/B)	$20	
D. If not, can you split your budget 80/20?	80%/20%	$1,600/$400
If so, how much per item will you spend?	20 @ $80 $1,600/20	80 @ $5 $400/80

Which items that meet the criteria in Table A will fit the budget you created in Table B?

Plus, keep in mind that this budget doesn't account for distribution. Perhaps your gifts will be hand delivered by your sales staff, therefore saving you additional costs. But if your plan is to mail or use a courier service to distribute the items to the audience, fulfillment costs must also be factored into the equation.

A promotional products advisor will fit the most suitable products to your budget in consideration of your target market, your distribution plan, and your desired outcome. Whether you're distributing a one-dollar "attention getter" to 50,000 people or a one hundred dollar gift to just ten people, it's important that your recipients feel great about the product.

Note: A copy of these tables is provided in Appendix A of this book

Chapter Six

Tips on Choosing the Appropriate Product

Okay, let's talk relevance. By now you know that effective promotional products are appropriate to your audience. It's also vital that the items you choose do not conflict with your business, industry, or image.

If your company markets beauty products, would you give your clients a plastic key ring? Would you deliver a refrigerator magnet to the CEO of a technology company? Would you send mouse pads to fishermen?

Each business and each application is different. These questions are simply aimed at helping you to think about what will work best for your project, your company, and your target market. You may be surprised at what will actually work for some promotions.

Let's Take A Closer Look...

If your target market is fishermen and your product is boating equipment you probably would not send a fluffy soft toy or computer accessory. But if you sent a floating can holder or inflatable key tag, the first thing they may do after reading your offer is to use the gift, and perhaps respond to your promotion within a few days, if not immediately.

Consider gender and environmental differences. Office workers will use a pen, mouse pad, highlighter, letter opener, or ruler, while a carpenter might rather have a builder's pencil, mobile-phone holder, pocket note pad, or tape measure. But don't make the mistake of sending a one-dollar tape measure to a professional builder. Save that for the "weekend-warrior" at the home improvement store and send the builder something of acceptable quality that he or she will likely use daily for many months, if not years.

If your recipient really appreciates and uses the gift, he or she will remember where it came from, and you'll benefit from increased customer loyalty for a long time. If you go cheap or gimmicky, however, the awareness will likely stay with the prospect for about as long as the gift – not long at all if relegated to either a child's toy box or the trash can.

So how do your ensure appreciation and usage? Carefully consider both the demographics and psychographics of your audience, just as you do for any other advertising medium you use. What are the ages, income levels, and locations of your audience members? What are their professions, hobbies, and personal preferences? It's likely you keep this information in a relationship-management database. When you share this data with your promotional products advisor, it can help to create a better, more targeted promotion and appropriate product for your audience.

You likely wouldn't choose an imprinted tank-top to influence a group of senior citizens. That might be better suited to a recording-label's incentive campaign geared toward students on spring break. And while an engraved magnifying glass in a velvet pouch might convince a retiree to "take a closer look" at information on a retirement community, it probably wouldn't do much to motivate a teen who lives with her parents.

In this example, a tank-top better reflects the youthful flair of the music company it touts. The magnifying glass shows the thoughtful attention to detail that a retiree would seek in a retirement community. Both these product examples show how a promotional item can be appropriate to *both* the audience it's intended for and the company that it represents.

Here's another example of how to decide which products are best suited to your promotion. Using Table C, in Appendix A of this book, will help to determine the appropriate product type to send to office-based managers of various ages. For the sake of this example, there is an equal mix of men and women.

Mouse pads, highlighters, clocks, calculators, pens, and photo frames would suit office workers, but in this case highlighters and mouse pads may not be suitable, if the gift is going to top-level management. Photo frames may not be the best option for young men, and pens might be favored by men more than women. While these are certainly generalizations, they are generalizations based on years of experience.

So of all the items on our initial list, it appears that the products likely to be most universally well received by the people in our target audience are clocks and calculators. Now we can consider what style, how much we will spend, how the item will be distributed, and whether we need to look at extra packaging ideas.

This is just one method to narrow down the options and identify the key considerations.

Table C - Choosing Audience Appropriate Products

Initial items of choice are rulers, pens, highlighters, note pads, mouse pads, desk pads, calendars, coasters, clocks, pen sets, photo holders and screen savers. Primary consideration by the client is that the gift is practical and best suited to the most people in the selected target markets.

Target Market	Mail Out	Hand Out	Functional	Looks Good
Male			**Clocks, Calculators**, Pens	
Female			Photo Frames, **Clocks, Calculators**	
Senior Citizen				
Teen				
Works in Office			Mouse pads, Pens, Highlighters, Photo Frames, **Clocks, Calculators**	
Works Outdoors				
Foreign				
Staff				
Executive			Pens, **Clocks, Photo Frames, Calculators**	
PA				
Factory Worker				
Accounts				
Sponsorship Team				
Prizes/ Awards				

If you take a few items that appeal to you and then write them into the sections that seem to be the most relevant, you'll soon discover that some things will work for everyone in your target audience! Some other column headings you could make include high visibility, low visibility, trade show attendees, sales staff, gifts-with-introduction.

Chapter Seven

Articulating and Reinforcing
Your Brand Values

So just who is your company, and what do you represent beyond your actual product or service? Understanding your brand values and clearly articulating those values to attract the right clientele is one of the keys to the successful use of promotional products.

In this chapter, we'll help you to apply this thinking in the selection of products.

What Does Your Brand Mean?

High Quality? Great Selection? Excellent Value? Unrivaled Service? These are just a few examples of how companies position themselves to be perceived by their prospects and clients every day. Ideally, these brand values also reflect the *desires* of the targeted audience itself.

For example, four wheel drive, luxury vehicle owners may ski or hunt, wear top of the line clothing, expect to travel in comfort and style, and want to look good while doing so. So when deciding between two types of promotional sports bags as a gift-with-purchase for a $100,000 vehicle, some deciding factors might be:

Brand Values	Rugged	Masculine	Stylish	Expensive Looking	Hard Wearing
Leather Bag	✓	✓		✓	✓
Canvas Bag	✓	✓	✓		

Factors such as top stitching, brass rivets, and extra pockets might add to the value of either bag, but one choice will likely demonstrate your brand values more effectively than the other. In this case, a leather bag may be more "audience appropriate" than its canvas counterpart.

Another example could be a budget stationery company, whose brand values are dependability, low cost, good quality, wide range and customer satisfaction.

Consider two different styles of pens. *Pen A* has been around for generations, a recognized, hard-working brand that is known to work on lots of surfaces. It's plastic, very low cost and available in 40 color combinations. *Pen B* is also plastic, but is new to the market. It has a gold trim, is a little flashy looking, and available in six colors. Chances are the gold will wear off after a while, but it may still be a pen style that people will perceive as being more expensive, and therefore a better value.

In short, both are good quality and will suit the company image. But when checking them against the brand values, one will be more suitable than the other for this particular company.

Brand Values	Customer Service	Dependability	Low Cost	Wide Range	Good Quality
Pen A		✓	✓	✓	✓
Pen B			✓		✓

Whatever your application, a trained promotional products advisor can help you to customize a product to fit your brand image. Maybe it's as simple as changing the imprint colors to an exact Pantone color match of your corporate logo and adding a tag line that touts your brand values or ties-in with your ongoing advertising campaign. Or customization could be used to create an exact product replica. Designs have been created to mirror everything from the Classic Coca-Cola bottle to an industrial chainsaw or a specific automobile model. Replicas may take the form of a keychain, mug, mouse pad… the list of options goes on and on.

Whatever you decide, never compromise your brand values. Recognize them, reinforce them, and refer to them when making buying decisions about any item that will carry your brand. Share insights about your brand values with your promotional products advisor and you may be surprised at all the relevant choices you have.

Chapter Eight

Corporate Gifts

This chapter looks at some of the do's and don'ts of successful gift-giving in business, both locally and internationally. In particular, how to avoid making cultural or relationship errors that can seriously affect your business.

During the holiday season, the promotional products industry kicks into high gear, keeping up with an ever-increasing demand for business gifts. Business owners, managers, and their personal assistants flock to promotional products advisors searching for something "different" that looks as if it's worth one hundred dollars... but costs around twenty!

A trained promotional products advisor can help you to determine what best suits your budget, company image, and the recipient's needs. In addition, he or she will pinpoint the products that can actually be obtained, wrapped and delivered in time to meet your needs and deadlines! To ensure your gifting program is as successful as possible, you'll need to consider the following questions:

What Are Your Reasons For Giving a Gift?

Is your primary goal to recognize the holidays or to say thank you for your clients' business? Are you more interested in acknowledging your clients for past purchases or providing a "gift of obligation," designed to encourage larger and more frequent purchases in the future?

Do you wish to thank the manager, chief executive officer, the accounts clerk, the purchasing officer, the personal assistant, or all of them?

If you send a gift to an entire company or division, a basket of treats or a large imprinted tin filled with popcorn for sharing are practical choices. You may also give the person with whom you do the most business a more personal gift.

However, in recent years, many companies have implemented strict policies that all gifts – including those offered to CEOs - would be put in a pool, and shared evenly among the entire staff. This is a fairly common way of senior management showing fairness to all employees in a company. If your gift list is short enough, it may be a good idea to ask your client's HR department about their gift policies.

If you do decide on a more personal gift, consider that some logo-bearing products tend to remain at the office. You may wish your gift to be something that is taken home and enjoyed daily. Coasters and glassware featuring prominent branding will likely stay at the office, while more subtle, personalized items, such as monogrammed crystal or a tone-on-tone embroidered golf shirt, are more likely to be taken home. You may also consider a more mobile option and look for a gift that can be used in the car, such as a stainless steel travel mug, or an embossed leather bag for traveling.

The decision also boils down to this important question: What is your objective? Do you want your client to see your brand as often as possible every day, or just when he is enjoying a particular pastime like a round of golf?

Furthermore, does your recipient expect your gift to be expensive? If she spends substantial amounts with your company each year, and you present a 39 cent stick pen, chances are she'll feel a little slighted.

> **Better to not give anything at all than to risk offending a key client by "cheaping out."**

Other Considerations

1.   Do you require special packaging for the presentation of your gift? Should it be boxed or wrapped? Will it be couriered, mailed, or hand delivered?

2.   If it is to be hand delivered, then by whom?

3.   Will you need to order a few extra, in case you run into any "last-minute" contacts or in the event someone overlooks a name on the list? What about clients who love your gift so much, they ask you for another one to give their boss?

4.   When are you going to give the gift? Will you be among the "Santa Parade" the week before Christmas, or would you benefit more by being first and sending it at Thanksgiving? A trend that is also becoming popular (and not just among chronic procrastinators!) is waiting until New Year and offering a *thanks for last year, looking forward to this year"* gift. Some businesses select other dates, such as the anniversary of their company, or the date a client began working with them.

Having a midyear special function, sale, or promotion, sending out cards, and inviting clients to stop by or call in for a free gift can also be a real winner.

Gifts For Overseas Trips and Foreign Visitors

In this multinational business environment, many managers and executives travel internationally on business. In so doing, the exchange of gifts to associates from foreign cultures is becoming increasingly common. However, there are certain cultural observations that should be followed if this practice is to be successful.

Some Basic Do's And Don'ts of International Gift Exchange

When In Rome – Do as the Romans Do

Follow the lead of your host, and don't be afraid to ask questions. It's often better to appear to want to learn the correct way of doing something than to assume anything and risk upsetting your associates.

For example, in most Asian countries, it's considered very rude to offer or receive a gift with only one hand – *use both hands.*

In some cultures gifts are meant to be displayed, rather than used. In western society, we often give and receive gifts that are intended to be useful, making pens and desk objects popular choices. Overseas, this type of product is best considered separately from any official presentation, because, especially in many Asian countries, high importance is placed on the official exchanging of more symbolic gifts.

Presentation Is Key

Don't just hand over gifts from your pocket as you grab your bags from the airport. Wrap your gift and make an important gesture in giving it. There are many choices available to enhance your presentation, from imprinted wrapping paper and tissue to embossed boxes or embroidered velvet pouches. Consider adding a personalized gift card, as well, tying your message of goodwill in with your corporate logo. Here is a perfect opportunity to show your client how much you value and practice attention to detail.

Don't Give Ice To Eskimos

Why take a gift to China that is made in China? A rich-looking desk-pad holder made in China may make a beautiful gift in the United States, but in its country of origin, don't assume that same blotter will be seen as anything but a cheap attempt at gifting. Instead, choose something that in some way incorporates the use of products made or sourced in your own country.

Take care not to deliver an insult, either. As mentioned earlier, it can be considered very rude to give knives or clocks in some cultures, as it may symbolize the cutting of ties or the desire to hurry your meeting.

Don't Risk Being Caught Short

It doesn't matter where you go, take a spare gift or two. You never know when you might need it. How embarrassing would it be not to have something to offer the additional senior executive or business principal that you weren't expecting to meet?

When attending a conference overseas, and taking a large number of gifts with you, it pays to check with officials (before you leave for your trip) about possible duty and import restrictions. You don't want to have to pay excess foreign dollars to get those fifty business-card holders and pen sets into your destination country. Customs processes can be time consuming and difficult. So first check the paperwork at home.

Know Your Regulatory Issues

Not only can regulatory issues regarding gifts vary from country to country, they can vary by industries within a country. For example, right now in the United States, a pharmaceutical company can no longer give a doctor a gift exceeding ten dollars. Strict limits are also imposed on gifts given by lobbyists to members of Congress. It often pays to speak with an expert on regulatory issues in the country and/or industries for which you're planning a gift, to avoid any hint of impropriety.

Chapter Nine

Packaging

While many promotional products and corporate gifts are given without packaging or in "ready-packaging," if you're trying to make a statement, interested in enhancing an image, or just want to improve on the basics, rethinking the packaging is a great way to start.

There are some very interesting forms of packaging available to increase the perceived value of a gift, and many companies that specialize in unusual variations. In this day and age, it seems that the old rules are gone; you can make just about anything work as packaging, thus adding impact to your gift. Even more important, packaging adds an interactive layer to your presentation, ensuring that the recipient spends more time admiring and opening the contents.

For example, a basic square box, creatively printed all over with instructions on how to open, and what to do with the contents, can be just as interesting as a very bright, colorful box with only the client's name and your company logo on it. Tie it up with ribbon, or wrap it in tissue, fancy wrap, comics or even plain old newsprint – whatever it takes to get the client (and hopefully everyone in the office) curious enough to put aside their task of the moment and open up the interesting package immediately.

Hint – it may be necessary to identify the package in some way either by ensuring your logo is visible or telling the receptionist about the product – just in case the recipient has any reason to feel overly cautious about it.

The promotional products industry offers everything from vinyl envelopes with floating sparkles and charms sealed inside to imprinted Mylar envelopes, burlap wine bags, etched metal boxes, cardboard firecracker mailing tubes, and more. Or you can have a special box designed or ask an industry plastics manufacturer to create a unique container. The right packaging might even linger in an office as a useful catchall, pencil holder, or decorative object.

Some promotional products even come ready to mail. For example, t-shirts can be "compressed" into custom shapes, shrink-wrapped with address labels and mailed like a postcard. When the package is opened, the T-shirt expands to full size.

You'll also find that packaging does not have to be custom or expensive. You can use plastic wrap, standard gift-wrap, pizza boxes, brightly colored envelopes, or just go wild with corrugated paper and raffia. Anything goes, and the way you present your product will also say a lot about your imagination, creative ability, and company image. These are things that many companies consider highly important when looking at spending their money. Your promotional products advisor will have many ideas to enhance your gift, extending the mileage of your marketing dollars.

Pay particular attention to packaging when targeting environmental groups, or even environmentally-conscious individuals (could be anybody!) I once shipped a package to a client in California, reusing some plastic bubble wrap that arrived in a package addressed to me. She called and asked how I could, in good conscious, send her a package with plastic bubble wrap in it. The fact that I was reusing (in my mind recycling) something that already existed in the world and would not increase the amount of landfill usage by one square inch did not placate her at all. So be aware that the inclusion of Styrofoam peanuts or plastic bubble wrap can mean certain death to even the best-intentioned gift. Instead, consider opting for environmentally sound, biodegradable cornstarch packaging or other environmentally friendly options.

When you do get creative with sending a gift, be sure to follow up with a call or email in a reasonable time after delivery to ensure that the package has been well received, and that all is well.

If you're sending a gift to someone and a more simple form of packaging is required, then consider at least putting your logo or marketing message on whatever packaging you decide to use. Finally, a gift card from you with a personalized note will also help to make a big impression.

It's relatively straightforward to print boxes, cards, wrapping paper, even tissue and ribbon – and while it's often readily discarded, it will certainly add to your professional image to go a little bit farther in your presentation.

Chapter Ten

Forging Business Relationships with Tax-Smart Strategies

Did you know that there are better, more tax-advantageous ways, to build business relationships than sending a bottle of wine or springing for expensive dinners, corporate weekends or special events? Let's look at some of the potential benefits of promotional products over other types of corporate gifts and the usual entertainment options.

Many companies offer a bottle of wine, host a corporate box at a sporting event or take a client to lunch, perhaps even on a trip, as a way of saying thank you for business.

While it's true that much business can be done on the golf course or over dinner, there are some disadvantages to this, especially when it comes to taxes and writing off the expense. This is not meant to suggest that you should stop entertaining, but simply to demonstrate that there are other options offering lasting benefits, which might make your accountant and bookkeeper happier.

Speaking of accountants, let's be clear here: you should always check with your accountant or tax adviser regarding any issues of business expenses and tax breaks. The authors of this book are not tax experts, and don't claim to be.

The primary point of this chapter is that you should examine where you spend your money, and what, if any, tax relief you might enjoy from adapting your entertainment and gifting habits to include promotional products.

According to the IRS, "you can deduct no more than $25 for business gifts you give directly or indirectly to any one person during your tax year." However, promotional products intended for marketing and advertising are often treated differently than traditional corporate gifts. Imprinted promotional products are often claimed as a general business expense from a company's marketing budget. As a result, they may not be subject to the $25 limit on business gifts and very likely do not fall under the category of entertainment expense, which may only qualify for a 50% deduction.

For example, if you were to give a client a wine connoisseur's set of opening devices and storage labels, with your company logo discreetly imprinted on them, is that set a promotional device (and therefore a general marketing expense) or is it a gift? That will likely depend on how, when, and why it's given. One thing is sure, however, the connoisseur's set will likely remain with the client much longer than a bottle of wine, providing far better residual marketing value.

You may choose to spend less on a bottle of red wine or port, but add a set of etched glasses or an attractive wine-knife to the package. A personally engraved corkscrew, with the client's own name, is likely to impress him even more than your fine selection from the wine cellar. And if the gift amounts to $25 or less, it might also impress your accountant.

When you choose to entertain clients via sponsored events, special dinners, or parties, look for ways to make the most of your investment by choosing promotional products to boost the power and remembrance-value of your invitations, party favors, and, even decorations and tableware. For a golf tournament, why not use imprinted golf balls? For a wine tasting, why not set out etched, corporate glasses? These logoed items may also be considered part of your general business and marketing expenses, depending upon exactly how they're used.

In addition to hospitality, you may be able to use promotional products cost-effectively in other areas—gaining PR mileage while avoiding tax penalties. Pens, note pads, and other office administration items can often be claimed as "administration expense" when used internally, or "advertising expense" when distributed to prospects or clients. Check with your tax advisor on how to get maximum advantage using the power of promotional products.

Chapter Eleven

Enhancing Your Image with Corporate Apparel

From caps and t-shirts to complete uniforms—making your staff easily identifiable can be a key part of your marketing—here are some ways to do this effectively.

If you use signs to identify your company buildings and vehicles, and printed stationery to identify your communications, then why not add corporate apparel and turn your staff into live, branded ambassadors for your business? Uniformed employees stand out from the crowd, and get your brand in front of more prospects and clients with walking, talking human billboards!

Uniforms can be used in a variety of ways. Here are a few examples:

- Frontline people in a retail store who need to be easily recognizable as someone who can help customers
- Behind-the-scenes staff who need to feel part of the team
- Delivery people who take your brand to the streets
- Employees socializing as a team after work
- Tradeshow staff, traveling together to your annual conference
- Even sports teams, branded with your logo through sponsorship agreements

Whether you provide uniforms for daily use or special occasions, this professional, branded look can enhance team spirit and present the desired image for your company. It can also provide a standard dress code, ensuring that each member of your staff is dressed appropriately for work. This has been a key concern for many HR departments in the wake of "dress down" policies run amok. The promotional apparel industry offers many choices in logoed business-wear and uniforms, from casual khakis and embroidered work shirts or polo shirts to logoed ties and even jackets.

In planning your company wardrobe, you can choose the level of dress required. You can also provide a range of choices to fit a variety of occasions, (i.e. a separate "uniform" for the office, trade-show floor and company baseball team.) The right garments will sometimes even spill over after hours.

For example, if you give t-shirts and caps to your staff or corporate-sponsored sports team, there's a good chance they'll eventually turn up at the gym or be seen at the supermarket or beach. This builds loyalty and a sense of community among your staff while also providing great, low-cost promotion of your brand!

Customizing Garments

When you buy corporate clothing, you have several options for customizing the garments including embroidery, screen printing, and transfer printing. It's important to note that your logo may not look exactly the same on all textiles, as it does on your company letterhead. For Example:

Version A
Company's Regular Logo

Version B
Modified for Embroidery

For example, a common problem arises with embroidering

detailed text. While this example is very basic, it illustrates a point. In order to get your message *noticed* on a cap or shirt, the best approach may be to avoid trying to replicate all the detail of your traditional logo. Instead, develop a slightly modified version of your logo, designed for *maximum visibility and impact* on clothing. In many cases, the bolder text will have much more impact. A trained promotional products advisor can work with you or your designer to adapt your logo for the best decorating results on apparel.

This is not to say that he or she will not honor your company's strict branding policies, however, in some cases a very slight variation may be required to achieve the desired results. We recommend that when you establish your brand guidelines and policies, you consider working with your promotional products advisor to ensure that your policies are in fact able to be followed in all ways when purchasing promotional gifts.

Another option is to have your logo transfer printed, which allows for finer detail, though it may not provide the look you want for your clothing. If all other clothing in your product range is embroidered, consistency may be preferred.

The following logo presents a different sort of problem:

ACME CONSULTING GROUP

Multicolored logos are sometimes more economical to produce as a transfer than a screen print. Not only will the details be more easily repeated via a transfer, you may find that if you want to regularly screen-print a multi-color logo in small quantities, the setup and production costs can be prohibitive.

Your promotional products advisor should be able to guide you through each of the options and help you decide upon the most suitable approach, based on your logo, the garment, job requirements, and your budget. He or she may ask you questions about the range of sizes and styles required for your staff, and make stocking recommendations based on that information.

Your representative will also consider what fabrics are needed for your work environment. For example, does the garment need to be stain-resistant and/or fire-retardant? How often will it be worn and washed (as this makes longevity and washability an issue)? Is the uniform for a union workforce that requires American-made apparel? Does the apparel need to be brightly colored, either for safety reasons or to help stand out in a trade-show crowd?

How long do you expect the garment to be a staple for your staff? Experienced promotional advisors know to check with suppliers on how long a particular style is likely to be available, so that when it comes time to reorder, you don't find that your staff's "signature shirt" is no longer available.

You may want to consider setting up a company store, where your staff and management can purchase corporate apparel and accessories. This makes replacing garments easy for employees, and maintains quality control over items selected by scattered divisions and/or franchisees.

Your promotional products advisor may also help your company develop a style guide, a written policy on how and where your logo is used (on clothing, stationery, promotional products) and the most cost-effective method of achieving a successful result.

Following is an example of a standard logo-reproduction and clothing policy form that a company might use.

Logo Use Regulations for Clothing – Example

ACME CLEAN

Acme Cleaning Company

Corporate Colors

- **"Acme" in PMS 032 Red**
- **"Clean" & Box in PMS 350 Blue**
- **On White background**

Logo must only be produced in the above colors, on a white background. If unable to be produced on a white background, then a white background must be printed as a third color.

Logo must at all times be produced with the blue box around the text. Text is to be centered with not less than 5 mm space around it.

Staff Clothing

Polo Shirts: Embroidered logo on left side chest, pocket size only. Names are to be embroidered on right side chest in white. All polo's must be XX Brand, royal blue – no pockets.

Shorts: Navy blue, cotton twill, not decorated.

Jackets: Blue and red anorak style, logo to be embroidered on left side above pocket. Company *name* only is to be embroidered across back in white.

Caps: Brushed cotton navy caps, with red sandwich peak. Embroidered logo on front of cap, and "Cleaning with Pride" embroidered across opening at back in white.

Note: Uniforms are not to be worn outside of working shifts.

Continued...

Logo Use Regulations for Clothing – Continued

Any employee who takes it upon him or herself to modify the wearing of the specified uniform without permission from the Marketing Manager will be subject to disciplinary action.

All uniforms will be supplied by ACME CLEANING CO, except for the shorts, which will be purchased by staff, and subsidized at $10 per pair. A total subsidy of $30 per year will be available to all staff members. All uniforms (along with security badges and identification cards) must be returned to Acme at the cessation of employment with the company.

All clothing items are to be purchased only through the corporate purchasing department, unless specifically authorized.

All logo reproduction, for all forms of marketing, must be approved in writing by the Marketing Manager.

Chapter Twelve

Maximizing Trade Show Response

In many companies, trade shows are a significant part of the marketing budget. Given their cost, the amount of time and effort they require, and their ultimate importance in reaching prospects and clients, it is vital to ensure an impressive return on investment. Promotional products, in conjunction with relationship marketing, are one of the most effective methods to boost your trade-show ROI. This chapter examines a few ways to use imprinted items before, during and after the trade show.

Send An Invitation They Can't Refuse

Prior to a trade show use your relationship-management database to create a list of clients and prospects that might visit the show. You can also contact trade-show management and ask if a mailing list of attendees is available. Once you have this information, plan a direct-mail campaign to advise prospects and clients that you'll be exhibiting, and encourage them to visit your booth.

Your promotional advisor can suggest products that may be delivered in two parts—the first as part of the direct-mail piece and the second redeemed at your trade-show booth. Or, you may choose a more expensive incentive for your top clients. This can be delivered at a scheduled meeting where you sit down with their representative during the trade show.

Dress for Success

You may choose to dress everyone at your booth in company colors and style. Whether clad in polo shirts and caps or business shirts with ties or scarves – your salespeople will be immediately identifiable with your brand, product and company name, strongly reinforcing your corporate image.

Also, when members of your team walk around the show, attendees will notice their presence, creating another subtle reminder to look for your exhibit.

Treat Them... and Improve Your Results

Make attendees feel special when they stop by to talk with you – when appropriate, have them sit down and offer them a drink or a treat. Refreshments can reduce barriers and increase concentration, and are often very much appreciated by tired trade show attendees. A simple idea that is always well-received is to offer chocolate or other candy imprinted with your logo.

Give Them Something to Remember You

Needless to say, you want to stand out from your competitors.

A low-cost item that is practical and useful, which gets your marketing message in front of recipients for days, weeks, or even months after the show, helps to ensure that you remain at the top of their "shopping list" when time comes to act on a purchasing decision.

Ideal for this purpose are key tags, magnets, stress balls, labels, giant paper clips, badge holders, staplers, rulers, pencils, pens, and drink bottles.

It's a good idea to keep a stash of imprinted products in various value levels, so that you can give a "lukewarm" lead a useful but less-expensive item, while offering a "hot" lead (or an important client!) a gift that is more appropriate to their value to your company. The key here, however, is being discreet so that no visitor to your booth is offended.

Be Mobile *And* Visible

Consider positioning extra staff or friends in company t-shirts promoting your booth number and special deals around the show. Highly visible balloons touting your logo and booth number, or useful, imprinted tote bags in the hands of show-attendees can further increase your presence at the show.

Another idea is to have an incentive promotion, for which staffers roam the show floor looking for attendees wearing a button imprinted with your company logo and booth number. The button may be included in trade-show gift bags, distributed at the door or mailed in advance of the exhibition. Those people found on the show floor wearing the button may receive a small gift, or perhaps be entered into a drawing for a much larger incentive. Such incentives encourage attendees to wear your company's "little billboard," thus spreading the word about your brand.

Manage Your Database - *Say "Thank You"*

After the show, send thank-you notes to all your qualified prospects, and include an invitation and incentive to contact you again. Send your post-show offer in the form of something that can be kept and used, such as a magnet or key tag, even if the prospects don't act on your offer immediately. A friendly gift in the mail is an extremely effective way to encourage prospects to talk with you further when you make a follow-up call.

Marketing in a show environment involves encouraging prospective buyers to first look at you, and then to *remember you* when the time comes to buy. Prospects that leave without buying on the day of the trade show aren't lost to you as long as you follow up promptly and generously, creating positive feelings about you and your company.

Chapter Thirteen

Your Promotional Products Advisor

In this book, you have seen numerous references to "trained promotional products advisors." The authors of this book have extensive experience with this medium, on two continents, and strongly recommend that you use a knowledgeable, established advisor when including promotional products or corporate gifts as part of your marketing plan.

Coauthor Maria Carlton conceived this book and published its predecessor in New Zealand as a way to help corporate buyers, small business owners and HR directors to get the most from their marketing investments. Simultaneously, thousands of promotional products advisors in the United States and Canada have received industry-specific training from coauthor David Blaise, either in person or via his *Top Secrets of Promotional Products Sales* Training System.

While the word "distributor" is the most commonly used term for those who recommend and sell promotional products, we have deliberately chosen *not* to use it here.

Clearly, there are some in the industry who do nothing but distribute products that are conceived, researched, manufactured, designed, decorated and imprinted by others. For them, the term distributor may be appropriate. However, the word is *highly inadequate*, and in that sense, *unfair* to those who have actually made a profession of creating, refining, recommending and delivering promotional *solutions* to the clients who need them.

Here are a few reasons that the authors believe a trained and qualified promotional products advisor is so valuable:

First off, the best advisors are acutely aware of the four factors of successful promotions and how to apply them to practically any market or industry. They're skilled at analyzing marketing problems and finding the right promotional product *solutions* to enhance the other components in your advertising platform.

They know which questions to ask, to help you get right to the core of your promotional issues. They provide you with excellent, targeted product recommendations that will have the desired impact on your prospects and clients.

They are well versed in the wide range of products available from thousands of industry suppliers, and they are knowledgeable about the methods used to customize, package and present these items. The best advisors in the world have developed a constantly improving supplier network, which helps to ensure that your product options are well made, imprinted correctly and delivered on time to avoid embarrassment or disappointment. In the event of a problem, your advisor's relationship with these industry suppliers can go far to save the day.

Using a trained advisor to help guide you, will save you time, money, and headaches.

The right promotional products advisor can also assist you in forming clear objectives about what you want to achieve, why you are promoting yourself, your products, your brand, and what the promotion is worth to you. They can guide you through a successful, cost-effective campaign.

What You Should Expect From Your Promotional Products Advisor

Some advisors specialize in areas such as corporate gifts, conference items, incentives, premiums, international gifts, novelties, imported items, or manufactured products. Some will have experience in many of these areas, knowing how to access nearly any product you can imagine. They take advantage of industry research tools that provide instant access to over half a million products from nearly 5,000 different suppliers. They can determine when and where to have your products manufactured to ensure you get the best results.

Make no mistake about it; these decisions are *critical* to the success of your promotion because *not all suppliers are created equal.* In fact, far from it. The most successful advisors provide objective information regarding the exact capabilities and qualifications of the suppliers they recommend and use.

In addition, they have the creative ability and know-how to come up with suggestions that are compatible with your own ideas and complement your other advertising and marketing programs. He or she may offer you "full service" to work through the many decisions you'll need to make in terms of budget, product type, quality and quantity, artwork, imprinting, fulfillment and ROI (return on investment) tracking.

An experienced adviser will be familiar with most of the different printing options (or at least know experts to consult), working with you to determine which method or methods best suit the product, logo, marketing message and project. The branding of any item is a very important part of the job, and should not be left to someone who lacks a clear understanding of how to do it well, and fully in accordance with your branding policies.

Most large companies have specific corporate-identity procedures stating how their company should be represented. Be sure to instruct your promotional products advisor about any such rules for your company.

Of course, honesty, integrity, and the ability to meet deadlines are always important key factors in providing peace of mind.

What Your Promotional Products Advisor Should Expect From You

When you find a knowledgeable, reliable promotional products advisor, it makes a lot of sense to *stick with them*. It takes time for people to get to know your company requirements, understand your corporate culture, establish payment terms, work out reproduction details of your logo, and do the adequate research to ensure that your job is being handled by the right supplier to meet your needs and deadlines. Don't try to rush through this process. As these elements fall into place, a good promotional products advisor can quickly become a very valuable and important member of your marketing team.

Companies that take a "disposable" attitude toward promotional product specialists by constantly bidding out projects to strangers and then buying based on price alone, often end up doing themselves more harm than good.

In an industry of 5,000+ suppliers of *wildly varying quality*, the quest for "cheapest price" often leads to botched print jobs, frayed nerves, missed deadlines and zero accountability. So while competitive price is always a consideration, be aware that the money saved during a grueling bidding process can be lost *many times over*, if the lowest bidder lacks the knowledge and resources to get the job done right or to help you recover in the event of a problem.

In every industry, those who are unable to sell their services based on skill, knowledge, quality or experience will invariably sell on price.

The best are rarely the cheapest, but loyalty to a reliable advisor pays enormous dividends by allowing you to avoid the grief, frustration, problems and embarrassment that often arise when doing business with those who sell based on price alone.

Chapter Fourteen

Saving Money, Time & Headaches with Artwork: How to Make it Easy on Yourself

It's important for your company image to ensure that your corporate brand or identity is always consistent, and you can save a lot of time, money and headaches by following a few simple guidelines when having your company's logo reproduced.

Working with professional people in any industry is always a good idea, particularly when you're having products printed to convey your corporate image. You have a much better chance of getting what you want, when you want it, and how you want it if the person you're working with knows exactly what they're doing. Promotional products advisors may have graphic art, digitizing or even imprinting capabilities themselves. If they don't have these capabilities in house, they may outsource or, in many instances, work with suppliers that include imprinting services as a matter of course. You can help them and yourself by providing your artwork in a way that ensures you the best results.

Art vs. Artwork

While art may be considered anything that is creative and artistic—from a simple crayon drawing on a napkin to a graphic drawn on the computer—*artwork* adheres to accepted guidelines and professional procedures (sometimes called standards) so that printers can reproduce it, either on paper or on a wide variety of promotional products.

When creating a new company logo, or even adapting your existing logo into acceptable file formats, it is a good idea to have your artist render additional versions as well. First, create the logo as envisioned, in full creative form, with all necessary colors. It is also very important to secure a paper copy that depicts the logo correctly and spells out each color exactly; these steps will help tremendously in insuring a quality print job.

Next, consider having your artist prepare several other acceptable variations.

Layout: If your primary logo or message is basically a square, consider creating a wider, rectangular version. It is much easier for the target audience to read one line on a pen than it is for them to roll the pen around to capture the whole message. Conversely, if your message is wide or tall, have the artist create more of a square-shaped version.

Additionally, create the logo or message with minimal information for use when imprinting space is at a premium. For example, you may want to create a version with and without your mailing address or your company's slogan or primary positioning statement.

Colors: If your company logo is made up of multiple colors, you should strongly consider also having a one-color version of the logo pre-approved as part of your authorized corporate look. The reasons are simple: some decorating options just may not be available if your logo is very complex and in multiple colors. For example, engraving on brass may only offer the option of being done in one color. Furthermore, it may be entirely too expensive to print your multi-color corporate identity on a low-cost promotional item. Do you really want the printing on your $1 pen to cost more than the pen itself?

Saving Artwork for Later Distribution

Ask your artist to save the logo or message in several electronic formats, and make sure they add your company name and contact information on each.

· **Vector Graphics File** is a method of image generation using a number of straight lines and/or arcs of different length and angular orientation. This format is highly recommended, as it offers the most flexibility and is used by most promotional product printers. Commonly used programs include CorelDRAW, Adobe Illustrator and Macromedia Freehand. Vector file format should be saved in its native format with embedded fonts and also as both an eps file and pdf file with fonts converted to curves or paths.

· **A Bitmap** is a digital representation of an image where a grid is used to indicate whether each point of the image is black, white or a color. If a logo or message has been created as a bitmap (or your existing logo has been scanned), save the file in its native format ie. .bmp, .tif or .pct. For this file to be considered acceptable, it must be at least 100% of the printed size for black and white images and 200% of size for color. Popular bitmap manipulation programs include Adobe Photoshop, and Corel Photopaint.

· **Metafiles** are a combination of Vector and Bitmap files. Metafiles can be acceptably used in some printing processes (but not all), and must conform to all vector and bitmap file standards.

Formats that are <u>not</u> recommended (or recommended for limited use):

· **Page layout programs** like Microsoft Publisher, Adobe Pagemaker or Quark Express are great for laying out ads, brochures and books, but are not well suited for transferring logos. Providing images in these formats will often result in additional artwork costs.

· **Word processing files**: Artwork created in Microsoft Word,

Corel WordPerfect or other word processing programs will usually need to be recreated, and will almost always incur additional artwork charges.

· **Home print programs** such as Print Shop Deluxe and others can acceptably print to a computer printer, but usually do not offer an acceptable way to transfer quality artwork for use on promotional products. These programs will also usually require a recreation of logos at an additional cost.

· **"Can't you just get the logo from our web site?"** Probably not. Graphics on web sites are designed to load as fast as possible, and usually lack sufficient quality for reproduction on promotional products. Can web graphics be adapted to work? Possibly. But it may involve recreating the logo, and will almost certainly result in additional costs.

Who Owns Your Logo?

To avoid possible copyright issues when contracting an artist to create an advertising logo or message, ask your attorney about a "work for hire" agreement that the artist can sign, stating that you and your organization are purchasing all rights to use, recreate and manipulate the logo or message.

Your promotional products advisor understands the need to be consistent and not do anything to compromise your logo reproduction. Sometimes there are practical considerations that they can point out, to avoid common pitfalls prior to creating a promotional product program.

If you would like more information on the promotional product industry's "Smart Art" guidelines, visit www.ppa.org.

Chapter Fifteen

Why Do I Have to Pay For That? Understanding Industry Charges and Buzzwords

Like most industries, the promotional products industry has its own unique terms and buzzwords. And even the most seasoned advisors may sometimes take those terms for granted, and fail to fully explain what they mean.

This chapter is designed to provide you with basic information that will help you to better communicate with your promotional products advisor and achieve the results you desire. It covers just a few of the most common terms and decorating processes. Keep in mind, this is an area that changes rapidly with technological advances. Your advisor can guide you through the maze of decorating techniques to ensure that your logo or message is presented in the most favorable manner.

A Quick Guide to Common Setup Procedures and Charges

- **Camera Ready Artwork** – the traditional reference to artwork that is complete and ready to use without further modification. "Camera Ready" often consists of a black image on white paper, exactly 100% of the printed size, on high-quality photographic paper. While many office laser printers are capable of creating acceptable results, most ink jet printers are not. Remember, the final result will depend entirely on the quality of the artwork.

- **Color Separations** – With multi-color artwork, there is a separate piece of camera ready art for each printed color, and registration marks on each sheet to ensure that all the colors line up to create the desired result.
- **Film** – Camera ready art is often scanned or actually photographed to create either a film positive or a film negative that may be used in the creation of a screen or die. It more closely resembles the film of an X-ray than the film of a small camera.
- **Spot color** - Each specific color of ink is printed right where it's needed. What you see is what you get. For example, if you are printing a three color logo of green, blue and yellow, only green, blue and yellow ink would be used.
- **Process color** - This process mixes the four basic colors of cyan, magenta, yellow and black (CMYK) to create nearly any color allowing for the appearance of a "full color" imprint, using just four basic colors of ink.
- **Electronic Artwork** – a computer generated file of artwork that contains everything necessary to generate color separated, camera ready art. See chapter 16 for further details.
- **Setup Cost** – The charge to make a job ready for production.
- **Color Match Charge** – the cost to mix inks to match a specific color. The industry standard for color matching is the "Pantone" or "PMS" color matching system.

How Do You Want That Printed?

Here is a brief overview of the most common processes used to decorate promotional products.

Screen Printing: Setup involves using a combination of light and chemicals, to "burn" your image into a pattern on the screen. The screens are then set up and registered, and ink is then physically pushed through the pattern in the screen to imprint your design on a promotional product. The ink may then be "cured" by running the printed item under a heating element.

- **Pros:** Screen printing is relatively quick, affordable and long lasting. It can reproduce fine detail, color matching, and can be used on many surfaces, including glassware and textiles.

- **Cons:** With spot color printing, each color requires an additional screen and/or set up, often resulting in additional charges. Process color printing is possible, but color separations can be very costly, and getting a correct, consistent finished result can be tricky. Flash curing individual inks may also be necessary when printing color on color (particularly white on dark items.) This may result in additional "flash" charges.

  Also, with some textiles, such as nylon, the type of ink available will simply not handle close color registration or multi-color layering. This can prove quite problematic when printing bags and umbrellas with complex logos.

Pad Printing: Setup involves rendering your image onto a rubber pad template, similar to a soft rubber "stamp." Ink is then transferred from the rubber pad onto the promotional product.

- **Pros:** Pad printing can be used to print on irregular surfaces, like golf balls or even walnuts. Color matching is also possible.

- **Cons:** Multiple color printing is not always possible, and pad printing is best suited to smaller imprint areas.

Embroidery: Set up involves telling an embroidery machine exactly where to place each stitch. Thread sewn into a pattern, creating the logo or message.

- **Pros:** Embroidery is perceived as an "upscale" option, providing a rich and sophisticated look.

- **Cons:** It is not always possible to reproduce fine detail or shading in an embroidered logo. In some cases, modification of the logo may be necessary. "Digitization," "punching" or "tape" charges (embroidery setup) can be more expensive than other types of setup charges. These costs are usually based on the number of stitches (i.e. larger designs mean more stitches and a higher price.)

Offset printing: Setup involves the creation of a plate or template. An inked image is set off from a printing plate onto a rubber blanket which in-turn is transferred to paper.

- **Pros:** The process provides exact reproduction, and is inexpensive in larger runs.

- **Cons:** Offset printing is limited to flat paper products.

Transfer Printing: In this process, transfers are created, utilizing special printers and sublimation inks. Heat and pressure transfer the image onto the promotional product.

- **Pros:** Full color is possible, and digital printing allows this to be done, even in smaller quantities

- **Cons:** Cannot be used on all surfaces. Limited to use on promotional products designed to receive sublimation inks (i.e. certain t-shirts, glassware, mugs, mousepads and plaques.)

Etching and Engraving: Setup may involve creating a template or programming the laser (or other equipment) on where to cut. In this process, a hand tool, chemical, laser or abrasive is used to remove material and etch or cut the logo or message into the product. This process can be used on a variety of materials including metal, glass, stone and wood.

- **Pros:** Beautiful, three-dimensional look.

- **Cons:** Setup can be costly, and no colors are involved, unless another decoration process is also used.

Hot Stamping, Embossing and Debossing: Setup begins with the production of a metal die, and costs can vary according to size. The die is used to press the logo or message into the promotional item.

- **Pros:** These processes provide excellent results on vinyl, leather and even some paper products.

- **Cons:** It is not always possible to reproduce fine detail or shading using these processes.

Chapter Sixteen

Promotional Products and the Laws of the Universe

For many people, creating a promotional products campaign is just a tiny part of their overall job description. In a small to medium sized company, anyone from a secretary to a CEO may be involved. To some, it may not seem like a very important aspect of their job. However, it's amazing how quickly it takes on a special importance and urgency, if it is not done correctly.

We live in a world of light speed communications with instant messaging, digital files, digital artwork, even digital signatures. And while the technology that allows these advances is incredible, it can sometimes lull us into a false sense of security.

When commissioning a custom imprinted job, we are often tempted to procrastinate. After all, if it takes just *seconds* for an email to travel half way around the world, how long could it take to imprint a twelve color logo on a few hundred folders?

The problem with this thinking is that it fails to take into consideration an important factor:

The Laws of the Universe Apply to Everyone

It takes time to create camera ready art, burn screens, make dies and imprint or embroider products. It takes time to transport merchandise from the manufacturer to the decorator, and from the decorator to you.

When it is done well and accurately, the creation of a successful promotional products campaign involves thoughtful consideration, clear objectives, strategic coordination and detailed communication of all those involved. It requires human and financial resources.

It also requires the cooperation of outside vendors, such as transportation companies, that may not appear particularly responsive or accountable to anyone.

Certainly, deadlines will always be a factor. But recognize that the laws of the universe continue to apply. Think the process through in advance. Allow adequate time to obtain the necessary approvals and provide your promotional products advisor with the materials, information and feedback to get your job done right.

Appendix A

Tables

Table A - Thinking About Products

Here are a few questions to consider when deciding which types of promotional products to use for your marketing:

	Yes	No	Maybe
Do I want many low cost items?			
Do I want fewer, high quality, higher priced options?			
Do I need a large imprint area to accommodate more than just a logo?			
Does the product need to last for more than a few days?			
Will it be distributed by hand?			
Will it be sent via overnight courier?			
Will it be mailed?			
Is my company and project suited to fun or unusual novelty items?			
Is the item likely to get in front of and remain in front of the decision maker?			
Should I be conservative in my approach?			
Do I want the recipient to keep the product for himself or herself?			
Do I want the recipient to pass the item on to someone else after the message has been read?			
Does it matter if the item breaks or looks worn after the campaign is finished?			
Should the item itself be useful and practical?			
Does the item need to prompt an action from the recipient?			
Does the item have sufficient perceived value to prompt such an action?			
Will the item be used to test the effectiveness of other media (i.e. print, radio or TV) and be used as part of a larger, integrated campaign?			

Your answers will help to give you and your promotional products advisor a clearer idea of how to allocate your budget.

Table B - Working from a Budget

Sometimes the easiest way to approach a project is to work backwards from the budget

Enter your responses below:

A. What is your maximum budget?		
B. How many items do you need?		
C. Are all recipients 100% the same? (If yes, available dollars per item = A/B)		
D. If not, can you split your budget 80/20?		
If so, how much per item will you spend?		

Which items that meet the criteria in Table A will fit the budget you created in Table B?

Plus, keep in mind that this budget doesn't account for distribution. Perhaps your gifts will be hand delivered by your sales staff, therefore saving you additional costs. But if your plan is to mail or use a courier service to distribute the items to the audience, fulfillment costs must also be factored into the equation.

A promotional products advisor will fit the most suitable products to your budget in consideration of your target market, your distribution plan, and your desired outcome. Whether you're distributing a one-dollar "attention getter" to 50,000 people or a one hundred dollar gift to just ten people, it's important that your recipients feel great about the product.

Table C - Choosing Audience Appropriate Products

Initial items of choice are rulers, pens, highlighters, note pads, mouse pads, desk pads, calendars, coasters, clocks, pen sets, photo holders and screen savers. Primary consideration by the client is that the gift is practical and best suited to the most people in the selected target markets.

Target Market	Mail Out	Hand Out	Functional	Looks Good
Male				
Female				
Senior Citizen				
Teen				
Works in Office				
Works Outdoors				
Foreign				
Staff				
Executive				
PA				
Factory Worker				
Accounts				
Sponsorship Team				
Prizes/ Awards				

If you take a few items that appeal to you and then write them into the sections that seem to be the most relevant, you'll soon discover that some things will work for everyone in your target audience! Some other column headings you could make include high visibility, low visibility, trade show attendees, sales staff, gifts-with-introduction.

About the Authors

David Blaise

David Blaise is an entrepreneur and business consultant with over twenty five years experience in direct marketing and advertising, with over a dozen of those years spent in the promotional products industry as a sales representative, sales manager, marketing manager, business owner, sales trainer and coach. He is the author of numerous sales and marketing systems on DVD video, audio CD and cassette, including *Sledgehammer Marketing* and *Top Secrets of Promotional Products Sales*.

Mr. Blaise is an internationally recognized speaker-trainer and a frequent contributor to many marketing and promotions related magazines. He is responsible for conducting all the full-day, new distributor training for the ASI Shows in Orlando, Dallas, Las Vegas and Chicago and he has also conducted education events for the Specialty Advertising Associations of Greater New York (SAAGNY) and California (SAAC), Document Management Industries Association (DMIA), Promotional Products Associations of the Midwest, Mid South and many others.

His *Sledgehammer Marketing* workshop on DVD and VHS video teaches marketers how to drive a steady stream of qualified leads to their door, convert those leads into sales, and retain the clients created in the process.

For details via autoresponder
Email: power@SledgehammerMarketing.com

For details online
Visit: www.SledgehammerMarketing.com/power

For details via phone
**Call Toll-Free in the US and Canada: 1-800-494-2721 Ext 130
Outside US, dial 1-610-685-9700, Ext. 130**

Maria Carlton

Maria Carlton comes from a marketing background that spans nearly 20 years working in the sales, advertising, printing, promotional product and media industries. She also owned and operated her own successful award winning promotional products company for nearly 10 years before selling it to commence her successful coaching and consulting career in 2001.

Her ability to come up with great ideas for promotions, marketing and advertising are enhanced by her incredible ability to see branding matters very clearly and identify valuable changes for most organizations. Her passion is in seeing businesses excel through good planning and working smarter not harder. Maria firmly believes that you can have it all and that you don't have to work 60 or 80 hours per week to do so. Maria combines good business and marketing ideas with balance and life-style ideas.

Maria was recently selected by a renowned USA publisher to be one of only a handful of business mentors to contribute to a book called *The World's Greatest Business Mentors*, due for worldwide release in 2004. She is one of only two people in Australasia to be included in this project and is recognized as one of the top 50 business mentors in the world.

Maria is a graduate of Coach University, and a member of the International Coaching Federation, and National Speakers Association. She is based in New Zealand, and has clients in Australia, USA and Europe.

For more information about Maria Carlton and to download a wide range of FREE articles, please visit www.compassnz.com

While there, you may also like to subscribe to her FREE monthly E-Zine, *'Navigating the Marketing Minefield'*. This is packed full of ideas for maximizing your business opportunities and increasing your marketing success.

You can email maria@compassnz.com, or you can write to her at P.O. Box 20469, Hamilton 2015, New Zealand. Phone +64-21-849 948

"I was quoted $15,500 to have an advertising agency do (in thirty to forty five days) what Sledgehammer Marketing allowed me to do in a matter of hours. It is easily worth twenty five times its cost."

Dave Wimer, President, High Foods Inc.

"How to Attract Qualified Leads to Your Door, Convert Those Leads into Profitable Sales and Retain the Clients You Create in the Process..."

Dear Fellow Marketer,

How much is just **one profitable new client** worth to your business? How much are ten worth? How about a hundred?

Suppose you could cut through the advertising clutter, reach *exactly* the prospects and clients you most want to do business with and create top of mind awareness with them... all for just pennies per lead.

Imagine you could do it with your own, completely customized, turn-key marketing system. That's right, a *system* that allows you to build your business predictably, *your* way! A system you can literally turn on and off at will. One that allows you to call your own shots, target the big-money, high margin clients you most desperately want to sell to and reach them with the most compelling marketing message possible about your business.

Isn't That About the Most Powerful Business Tool You Could Ever Possess?

Instead of knocking yourself out trying to put it all together, you can *have it all right now*, inside a revolutionary new system called:

Essentials of...
SLEDGEHAMMER MARKETING
"How to Drive Home Powerful, Targeted Marketing with Maximum Impact"

Join *Power of Promotional Products* coauthor David Blaise as he pulls back the curtain and reveals the information you need right now, to drive a steady stream of qualified leads to your door, convert those leads into profitable sales and retain the clients you create in the process.

If you're ready to stop reading and *start taking action* to create a marketing system that produces financial results for yourself and your family, begin your risk-free trial of *Sledgehammer Marketing* today.

Readers of this book save $50.00 if you act now!

For details via autoresponder: **Email power@SledgehammerMarketing.com**
For details online: **Visit www.SledgehammerMarketing.com/power**
For details via phone: **Call 1-800-494-2721 Ext. 130**